HAL•LEONARD

ESSENTIAL SONGS

PIANO VOCAL GUITAR

The 1990s

ISBN 0-634-09100-X

HAL•LEONARD®
CORPORATION
7777 W. BLUEMOUND RD. P.O. BOX 13819 MILWAUKEE, WI 53213

Visit Hal Leonard Online at
www.halleonard.com

CIVIC CENTER

CONTENTS

w: th (BABY FACE)

177	I Finally Found Someone	Barbra Streisand and Bryan Adams	8	1996
200	I Need to Know	Marc Anthony	3	1999
205	I Touch Myself	Divinyls	4	1991
210	I Will Buy You a New Life	Everclear	33	1998
218	I Will Remember You	Sarah McLachlan	65	1995
223	I Wish It Would Rain	Phil Collins	3	1990
228	If I Ever Fall in Love	Shai	2	1993
232	If You Had My Love	Jennifer Lopez	1	1999
246	Insensitive	Jann Arden	12	1996
252	Ironic	Alanis Morissette	4	1996
239	It's All Coming Back to Me Now	Celine Dion	2	1996
258	Let Her Cry	Hootie & The Blowfish	9	1995
262	Life Is a Highway	Tom Cochrane	7	1992
269	Livin' La Vida Loca	Ricky Martin	1	1999
276	(Can't Live Without Your) Love and Affection	Nelson	1	1990
284	Love Will Keep Us Alive	Eagles	22	1995
288	Lovefool	The Cardigans	2	1997
292	More Than Words	Extreme	1	1991
298	No Rain	Blind Melon	20	1993
305	Only Happy When It Rains	Garbage	55	1996
310	Right Here, Right Now	Jesus Jones	2	1991
324	Run Around	Blues Travelers	8	1995
315	Semi-Charmed Life	Third Eye Blind	4	1997
332	Silent Lucidity	Queensryche	9	1991
340	Smells Like Teen Spirit	Nirvana	6	1992
350	Stay	Lisa Loeb	1	1994
356	Superstar	Lauryn Hill	1	1998
362	That Thing You Do!	The Wonders	41	1996
366	This Kiss	Faith Hill	7	1998
370	Two Princes	Spin Doctors	7	1993
345	Under the Bridge	Red Hot Chili Peppers	2	1992
376	Walking in Memphis	Marc Cohn	13	1991
386	You're Still the One	Shania Twain	2	1998
390	Zoot Suit Riot	Cherry Poppin' Daddies	41	1998

ALL BY MYSELF

Music by SERGEI RACHMANINOFF
Words and Additional Music by ERIC CARMEN

When I was young, ___ I nev-er need-ed an-y-one, ___ and mak-ing love was just ___ for fun. ___ Those days ___ are gone. ___

poco rit.

ALL FOR YOU

Words and Music by KEN BLOCK, JEFF BERES,
ANDREW COPELAND, RYAN NEWELL
and MARK TROJANOWSKI

(1., D.S.) Fin-'lly I fig-ured out, but it took ___ a long, long time. ___

(2.) I thought I'd seen it all 'cause it's been ___ a long, long time. ___

Now ___ there's a turn-a-bout, ___ may-

Oh, ___ but then we'll trip and fall, won-

-be 'cause ___ I'm try-ing.}

-d'ring if ____ I'm blind. ____}

There's _ been times _

Fin - 'lly I fig -

D.S. al Coda

CODA

hard to say ___ what it is ___ I see ___ in you. ___

ALL 4 LOVE

Words and Music by ISAAC HAYES,
STEVE CROPPER, HOWARD THOMPSON,
BRYAN KYETH ABRAMS, MARK CALDERON,
SAM WATTERS and KEVIN KRAIG THORNTON

ALWAYS

Words and Music by
JON BON JOVI

Well, there ain't no luck ___ in these

when I die ___ you'll be on my mind ___ and I'll love you,

al - ways.

Guitar solo - ad lib. and Fade

Repeat ad lib. and Fade

Lead vocal ad lib.

ALWAYS BE MY BABY

Words and Music by MARIAH CAREY,
JERMAINE DUPRI and MANUEL SEAL

We were as one,__ babe, for a mo-ment in ____ time.
I ain't gon-na cry,__ no, and I won't beg you to ____ stay.__

BABY BABY

Words and Music by AMY GRANT
and KEITH THOMAS

BACK AT ONE

Words and Music by
BRIAN McKNIGHT

Slowly

It's un-de-ni-a-ble, that we should be ___ to-geth- er.
It's so in-cred-i-ble, the way things work ___ them-selves ___ out.

It's un-be-liev-a-ble how I used to say ___ that I'd ___ fall nev-er.
And all e-mo-tion-al, once you know what ___ it's all a-bout, ___ hey.

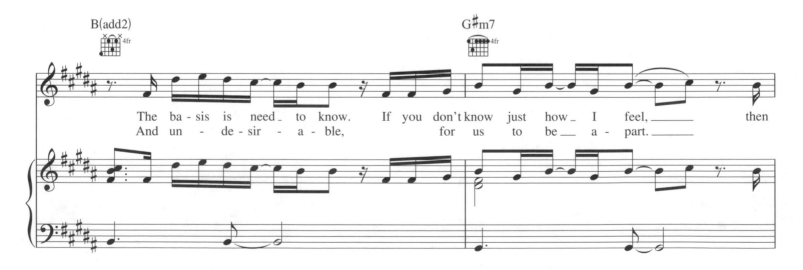

The ba-sis is need ___ to know. If you don't know just how ___ I feel, _____ then
And un-de-sir-a-ble, for us to be ___ a-part. ___

BLAZE OF GLORY

Words and Music by
JON BON JOVI

Moderate Rock

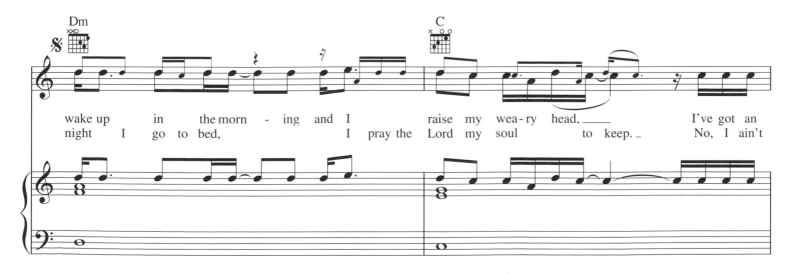

wake up in the morn - ing and I raise my wea-ry head,___ I've got an

night I go to bed, I pray the Lord my soul to keep.___ No, I ain't

no one's son. Call me young _ gun.

dev - il's son. Call me young _

You

gun.

Guitar solo ad lib.

Play 3 times

Solo ends

BECAUSE OF YOU

Words and Music by ARNTHOR BIRGISSON,
CHRISTIAN KARLSSON, PATRICK TUCKER
and ANDERS SVEN BAGGE

Blue

Words and Music by
BILL MACK

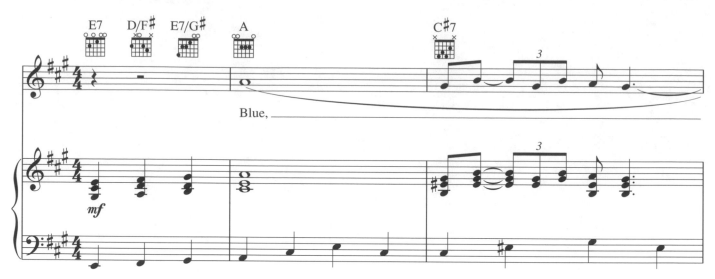

BRICK

Words and Music by BEN FOLDS
and DARREN JESSEE

CAN YOU FEEL THE LOVE TONIGHT

from Walt Disney Pictures' THE LION KING

Music by ELTON JOHN
Lyrics by TIM RICE

72

CHANGE THE WORLD

Words and Music by WAYNE KIRKPATRICK,
GORDON KENNEDY and TOMMY SIMS

78

COME TO MY WINDOW

Words and Music by
MELISSA ETHERIDGE

Come to my win - dow. Crawl in - side, wait by the light of the moon.

Come to my win - dow. I'll be home soon.

CRADLE OF LOVE

Words and Music by DAVID WERNER
and BILLY IDOL

DON'T SPEAK

Words and Music by ERIC STEFANI
and GWEN STEFANI

DON'T TURN AROUND

Words and Music by DIANE WARREN
and ALBERT HAMMOND

Reggae Pop

leave, _____ I won't beg you to stay. ___
arms   a - round me   hold - ing me tight. ___

And if you got - ta
And if you ev - er

go, _____ dar - lin', may - be it's bet - ter that way.
think _____ a - bout me   just know that I'll be al - right. ___

I'm gon - na be strong,
I'm gon - na be strong,

DREAMS

Lyrics by DOLORES O'RIORDAN
Music by DOLORES O'RIORDAN and NOEL HOGAN

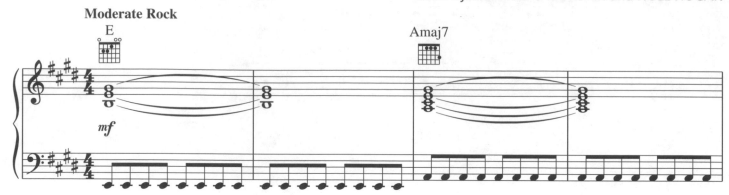

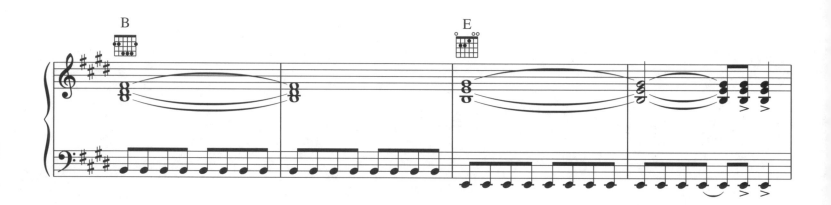

105

ESCAPADE

Words and Music by JAMES HARRIS III,
TERRY LEWIS and JANET JACKSON

Medium Dance groove

(Everything I Do)
I DO IT FOR YOU

from the Motion Picture ROBIN HOOD: PRINCE OF THIEVES

Words and Music by BRYAN ADAMS,
ROBERT JOHN LANGE and MICHAEL KAMEN

EXHALE

(Shoop Shoop)

from the Original Soundtrack Album WAITING TO EXHALE

Words and Music by
BABYFACE

Easy R&B Ballad

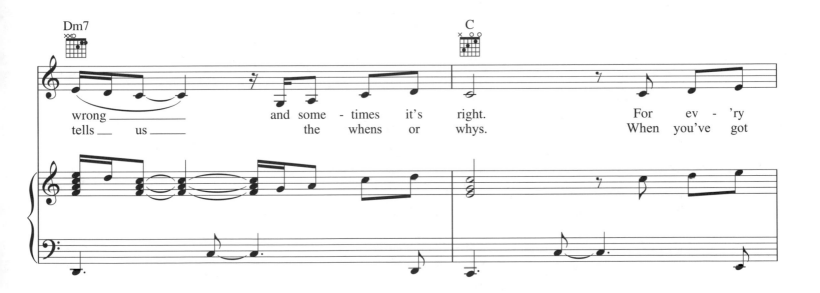

121

FIELDS OF GOLD

Music and Lyrics by
STING

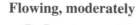

You'll re-mem-ber me when the west wind moves ___ up a-
stay with me, when will you be my love ___ a-

on the fields ___ of bar - ley. You'll for-get the sun in his
mong the fields ___ of bar - ley? We'll for-get the sun in his

FROM A DISTANCE

Words and Music by
JULIE GOLD

From a

heart _____ of ev - 'ry ___ man. _____ It's the

hope of ___ hopes, __ it's the love of ___ loves. __ This is the song ___ of ___ ev - 'ry

FREE AS A BIRD

Words and Music by JOHN LENNON,
PAUL McCARTNEY, GEORGE HARRISON
and RINGO STARR

thing   to   be _____   free __ as a   bird.
bird   I   fly, _____   as a bird on   wings.

To Coda ⊕

Whatever happened to __
the life that we once knew?   Can we real-ly live with-out   each   oth - er?

Where did we lose _ the touch _   that seemed to mean _ so much?   It al-ways made   me

GENIE IN A BOTTLE

Words and Music by STEVE KIPNER,
DAVID FRANK and PAM SHEYNE

Medium beat

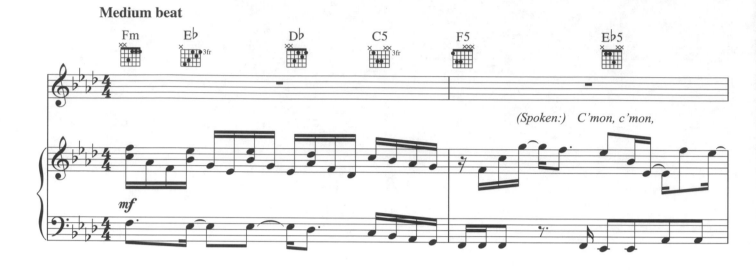

(Spoken:) C'mon, c'mon,

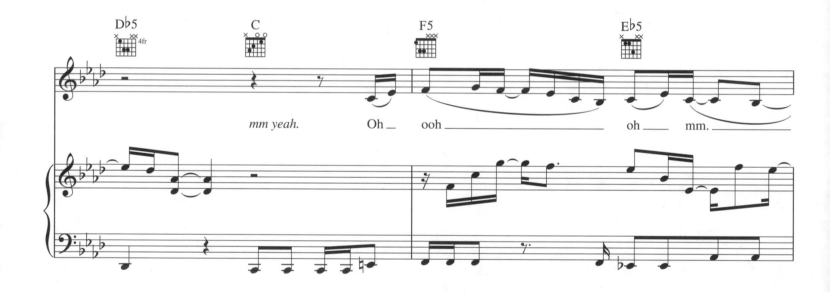

mm yeah.   Oh ___ ooh _____ oh ___ mm.

I feel like I've ___ been locked ___ up tight ___ for a cen-
Mu-sic's play-ing and the light's down low. ___ Just one ___

138

Oh. _____ But my heart is say-ing no, no.

If you wan-na be with me, ba - by, there's a price to pay. I'm a ge - nie in a bot-

-tle; you got - ta rub me the right way. If you wan - na be with

me, I can make your wish come true. You got - ta make a big __ im - pres-

140

GIVE ME ONE REASON

Words and Music by
TRACY CHAPMAN

Medium Blues

Tune guitar down one half step.

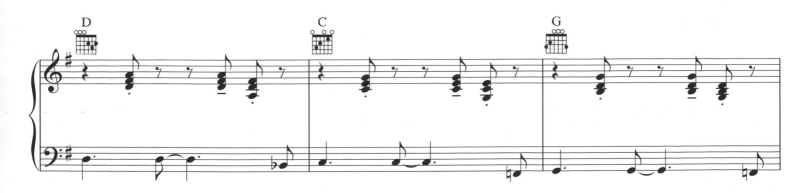

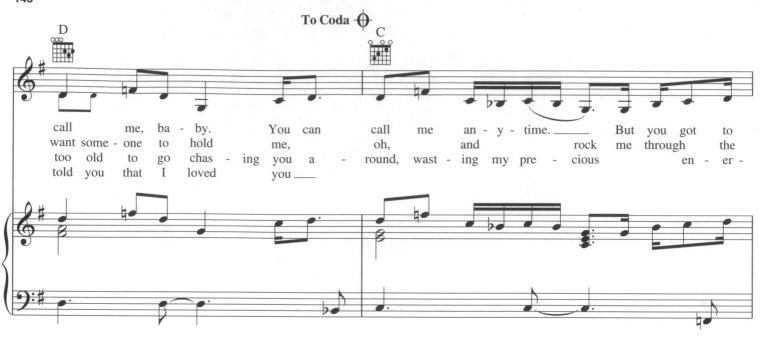

call me, ba - by. You can call me an - y - time. _____ But you got to
want some - one to hold me, oh, and rock me through the
too old to go chas - ing you a - round, wast - ing my pre - cious en - er -

call _____ me.
night. _____
gy. _____

(You could see me turn - ing.)

HAVE I TOLD YOU LATELY

Words and Music by
VAN MORRISON

Slowly, with expression

HOW BIZARRE

Words and Music by ALAN JANSSON
and PAUL FUEMANA

Spoken: Brother

Pele's in the back,   sweet Zina's in the front,   cruising down the freeway in the hot, hot sun.
T V news and cameras,   there's choppers in the sky.   Marines, police, reporters ask, "Where, for and why."

154

156

THE HEART OF THE MATTER

Words and Music by JOHN DAVID SOUTHER,
DON HENLEY and MIKE CAMPBELL

Moderately slow

I got the call _ to-day, I didn't want to hear _ but I knew that it _ would come. _
(See additional lyrics)

An old, _ true friend of ours _ was talk-in' on _ the phone, _ she said you

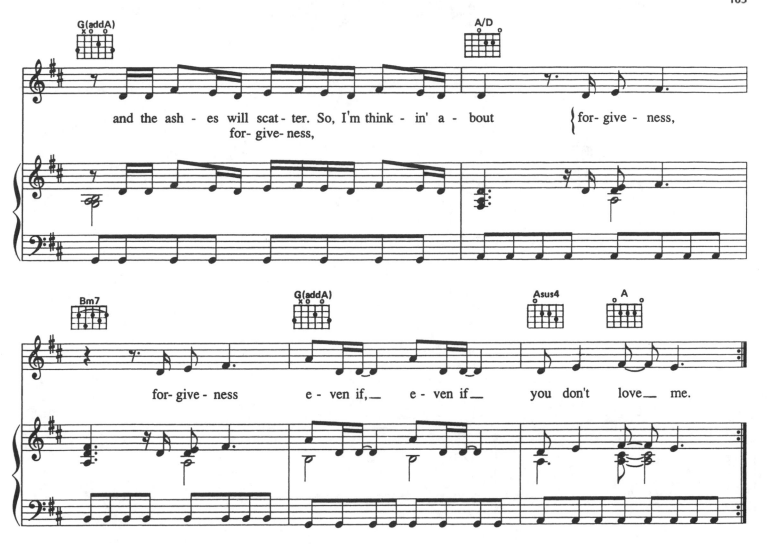

and the ash - es will scat - ter. So, I'm think - in' a - bout
for- give - ness,
{ for- give - ness,

for- give - ness   e - ven if,__   e - ven if__   you don't   love__ me.

Additional Lyrics

Verse 2:   These times are so uncertain
There's a yearning undefined
... people filled with rage
We all need a little tenderness
How can love survive in such a graceless age?
The trust and self-assurance that lead to happiness
They're the very things we kill, I guess
Pride and competition
    cannot fill these empty arms
And the work I put between us
    doesn't keep me warm

Chorus 2:   I'm learning to live without you now
But I miss you, baby
The more I know, the less I understand
All the things I thought I'd figured out
I have to learn again
I've been trying to get down
    to the heart of the matter
But everything changes
    and my friends seem to scatter
But I think it's about forgiveness
Forgiveness
Even if, even if you don't love me anymore.

HOLD ON

Words and Music by CARNIE WILSON,
CHYNNA PHILLIPS and GLEN BALLARD

169

I BELIEVE

Words and Music by JEFFREY PENCE,
ELIOT SLOAN and MATT SENATORE

Moderately, not too fast

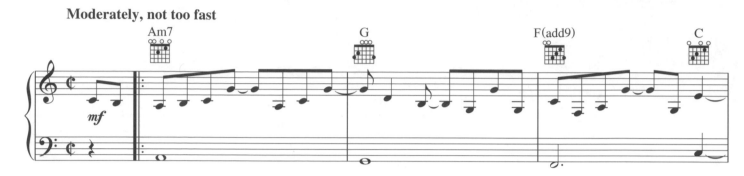

Walk blind - ly to _____ the light _____ and reach out for _____ his hand.
Vi - o - lence has spread _____ world wide and there's fam -'lies on _____ the street.
I've been see - ing Lis - a now for a lit - tle o - ver a year.

love will find __ a way. __

D.S. al Coda

I FINALLY FOUND SOMEONE

from THE MIRROR HAS TWO FACES

Words and Music by BARBRA STREISAND,
MARVIN HAMLISCH, R.J. LANGE
and BRYAN ADAMS

I CAN'T MAKE YOU LOVE ME

Words and Music by MIKE REID
and ALLEN SHAMBLIN

Turn down the __ lights, __ turn down __ the bed, __ turn down these voic - es in - side my head. __ Lay down with me, __

I DON'T HAVE THE HEART

Words and Music by ALLAN RICH
and JUD FRIEDMAN

191

I DON'T WANT TO WAIT

Words and Music by
PAULA COLE

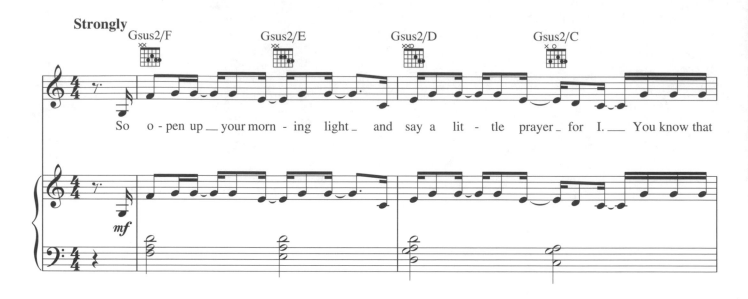

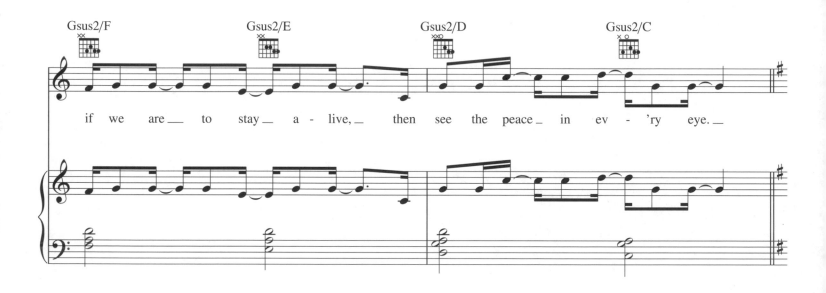

So o-pen up your morn-ing light and say a lit-tle prayer for I. You know that

if we are to stay a-live, then see the peace in ev-'ry eye.

Du du du du du, du du du du du,

195

I NEED TO KNOW

Words and Music by CORY ROONEY
and MARC ANTHONY

* *Recorded a half step higher.*

I TOUCH MYSELF

Words and Music by BILLY STEINBERG,
TOM KELLY, CHRISTINE AMPHLETT and MARK McENTEE

I WILL BUY YOU A NEW LIFE

Words by ART ALEXAKIS
Music by ART ALEXAKIS and EVERCLEAR

Here is the mon-ey that I owe you, yes, so you can pay the bills.

I will give you more __ when I __ get paid __ a - gain. __

I hate those peo-ple who love to tell you, _ "Mon-ey is the root of all __ that kills."

213

I WILL REMEMBER YOU
Theme from THE BROTHERS McMULLEN

Words and Music by SARAH McLACHLAN,
SEAMUS EGAN and DAVE MERENDA

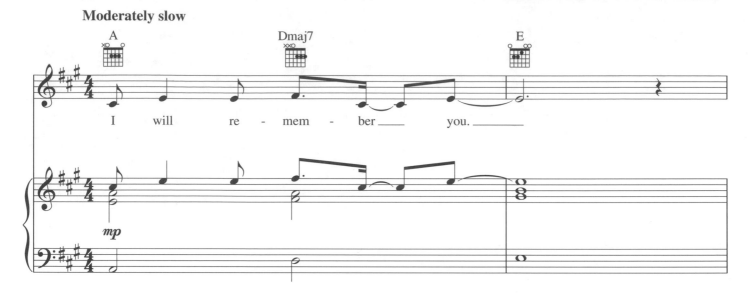

I will re- mem- ber you.

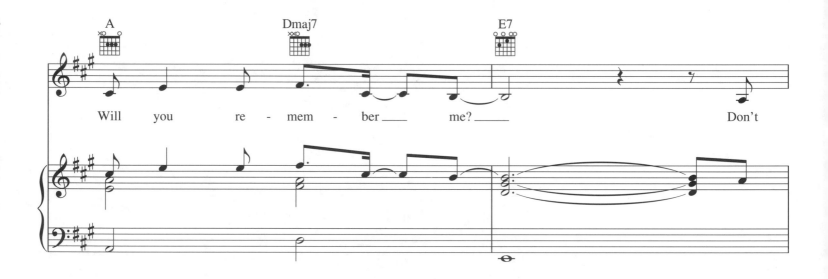

Will you re- mem- ber me? Don't

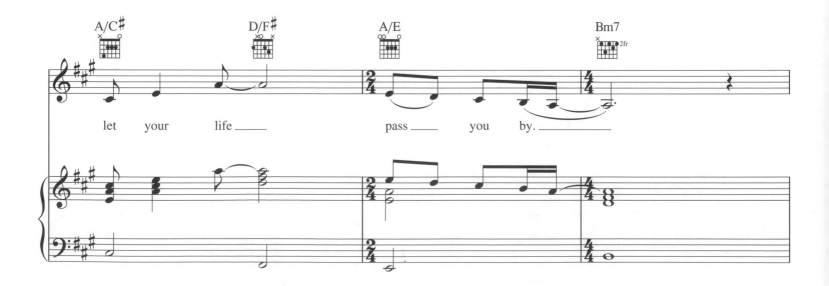

let your life pass you by.

222

I WISH IT WOULD RAIN

Words and Music by
PHIL COLLINS

Moderately

VERSE

You know I ne-ver meant to see you a-gain, ___ and I

See lyrics for verses 2 & 3 (%)

on-ly passed by as a friend, ___

226

VERSE 2:
You said you didn't need me in your life,
Oh I guess you were right,
Ooh I never meant to cause you no pain,
But it looks like I did it again.

VERSE 3:
'Cos I know, I know I never meant to cause you no pain,
And I realise I let you down,
But I know in my heart of hearts,
I know I'm never gonna hold you again.

IF I EVER FALL IN LOVE

Words and Music by
CARL MARTIN

IF YOU HAD MY LOVE

Words and Music by RODNEY JERKINS,
LaSHAWN DANIELS, CORY ROONEY,
FRED JERKINS and JENNIFER LOPEZ

Moderate steady beat

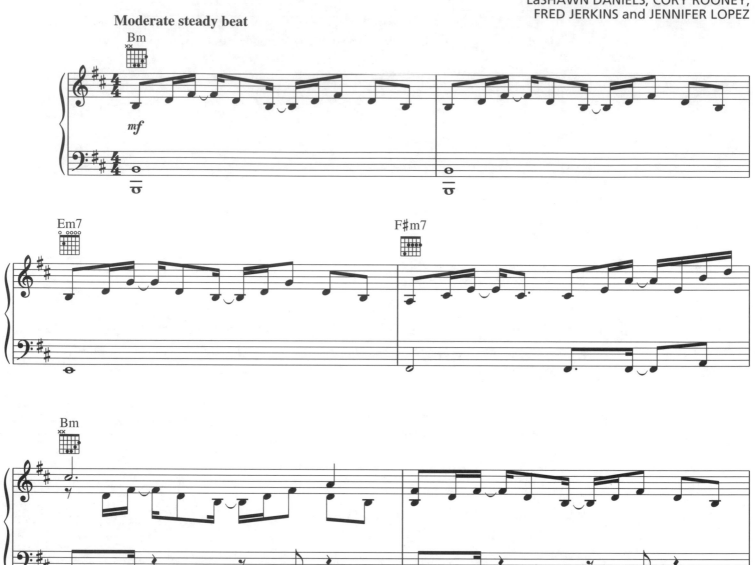

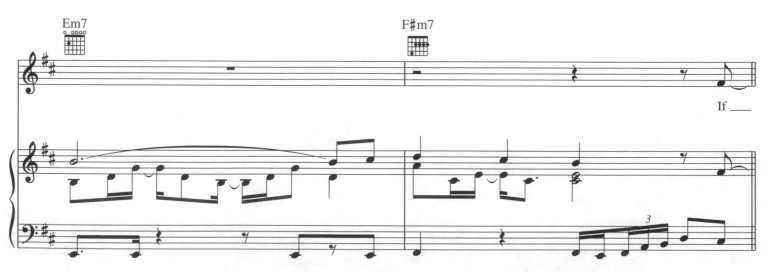

IT'S ALL COMING BACK TO ME NOW

Words and Music by
JIM STEINMAN

242

INSENSITIVE

Words and Music by
ANNE LOREE

How do you cool ___ your lips
How do you numb ___ your skin

IRONIC

Lyrics by ALANIS MORISSETTE
Music by ALANIS MORISSETTE
and GLEN BALLARD

LET HER CRY

Words and Music by DARIUS CARLOS RUCKER,
EVERETT DEAN FELBER, MARK WILLIAM BRYAN
and JAMES GEORGE SONEFELD

Moderately slow Rock

She sits a - lone by a lamp - post ____

try'n to find a thought that's es - caped ___ her mind. ____ She says, "Dad's ___ the one I ___ love ___

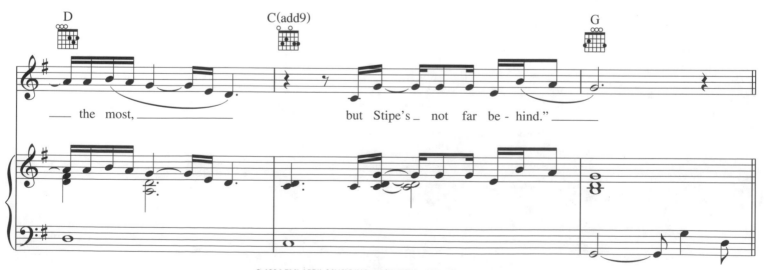

___ the most, _____ but Stipe's ___ not far be - hind." _____

261

LIFE IS A HIGHWAY

Words and Music by
TOM COCHRANE

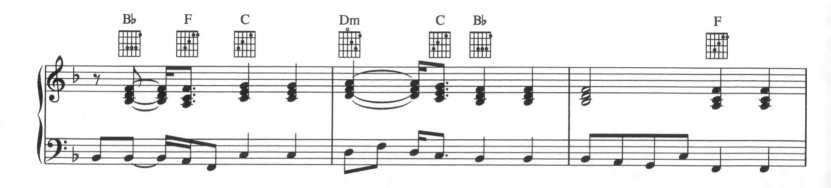

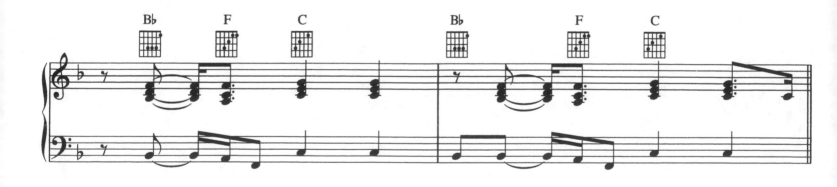

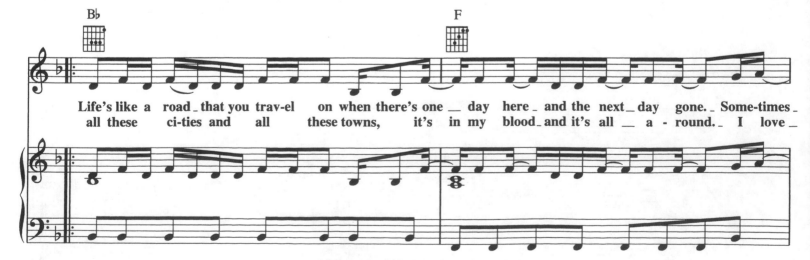

Life's like a road _ that you trav-el on when there's one _ day here _ and the next _ day gone. _ Some-times _
all these ci-ties and all these towns, it's in my blood _ and it's all _ a-round. _ I love _

LIVIN' LA VIDA LOCA

Words and Music by ROBI ROSA
and DESMOND CHILD

Fast, with a steady beat

She's in - to su - per - sti - tions, black cats and voo - doo dolls. __ I feel a prem - o - ni - tion. That girl's gon - na make me fall. __

(Can't Live Without Your)
LOVE AND AFFECTION

Words and Music by MARC TANNER,
MATT NELSON and GUNNAR NELSON

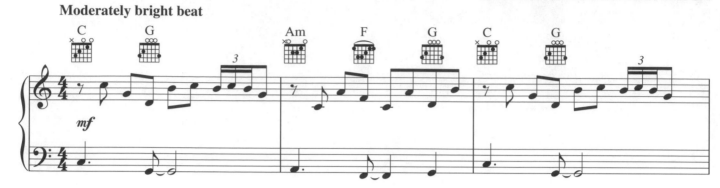

Here ___ she comes, mm, ___
goes. No,
wait, mm, ___

___ just like an an-gel. ___ Seems like for-ev-er that she's
she don't know what she's miss-ing. Can't ___ she see I'll nev-er
___ here for an an-swer. ___ Won-der if to-mor-row will be

been on ___ my mind.
give up ___ the fight.
like this ___ to - day.

Noth - ing has changed, she
I'll do all I can.
I keep hold - ing on,

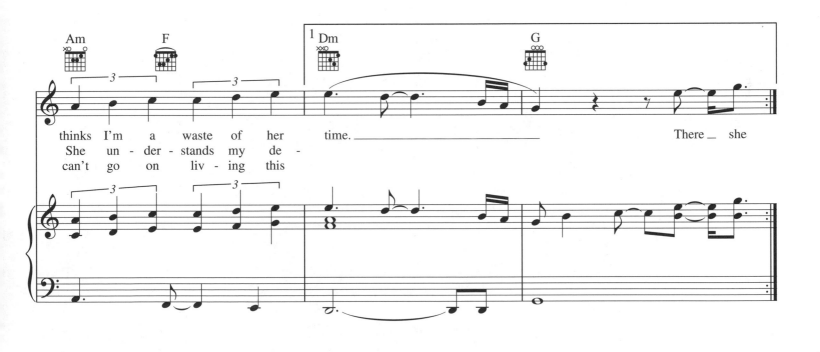

thinks I'm a waste of her time. ___
She un - der - stands my de -
can't go on liv - ing this

There ___ she

sire. ___
way, ___

ba - by. ___

I've been on the out -
I've been on the out -

LOVE WILL KEEP US ALIVE

Words and Music by PETER VALE,
JIM CAPALDI and PAUL CARRACK

LOVEFOOL

Music by PETER SVENSSON
Lyrics by NINA PERSSON
and PETER SVENSSON

MORE THAN WORDS

Words and Music by NUNO BETTENCOURT
and GARY CHERONE

* Recorded a half step lower.

NO RAIN

Words and Music by
BLIND MELON

All I can say ____ is that my life is pret-ty plain, ____ I

301

Guitar solo - ad lib.

All I can say ___ is that my life is pret-ty plain, ___ you don't like my point of view, ___ you think that I'm in - sane. It's ___ not sane, _____ it's ___ not sane. _____

ONLY HAPPY WHEN IT RAINS

Words and Music by DUKE ERIKSON,
SHIRLEY ANN MANSON, STEVE MARKER
and BUTCH VIG

Recorded a half step higher.

pour your mis - er - y down __ on me. __

Instrumental ends

I'm on - ly hap - py when it

I on - ly smile __ in the

dark. ____

My on - ly com - fort is the

night gone black. __

I did - n't ac - ci - den - tal - ly

RIGHT HERE, RIGHT NOW

Words and Music by
JESUS JONES

SEMI-CHARMED LIFE

Words and Music by
STEPHAN JENKINS

va - tion,   her own   mo - ti - va - tion.   She comes round   and   she   goes   down   on me.
back there smil-ing in the pic-tures you would take.   Do-ing crys-tal meth will lift you up un - til you break. It won't

To Coda ⊕

And I'll make you smile, like a   drug   for you.   Do ev - er what you want to do, com-ing o - ver
stop,   I won't   come   down.   I keep stock with the tick - tock rhy-thm,   a bump for the   drop, and then I

you.   Keep on   smil - ing what we go through.   One   stop   to the rhy-thm that di - vides   you.

And I speak to you __ like the cho - rus to the verse.   Chop an - oth - er line   like a co - da with a

RUN AROUND

Words and Music by
JOHN POPPER

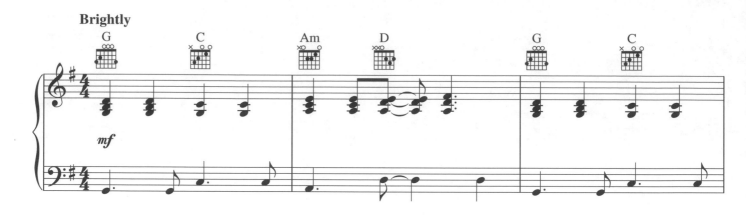

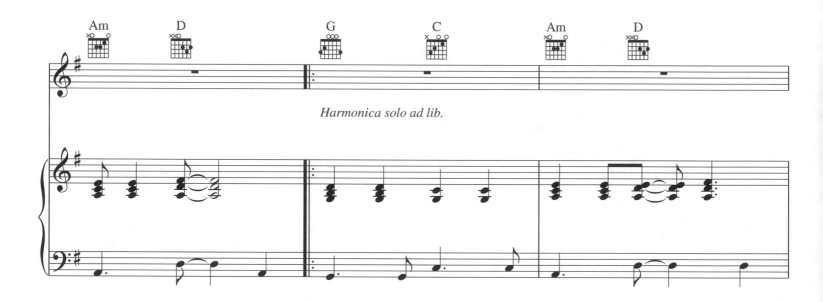

Harmonica solo ad lib.

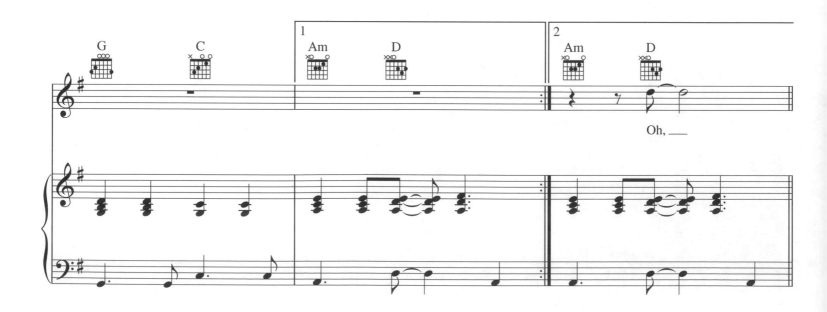

Oh, ___

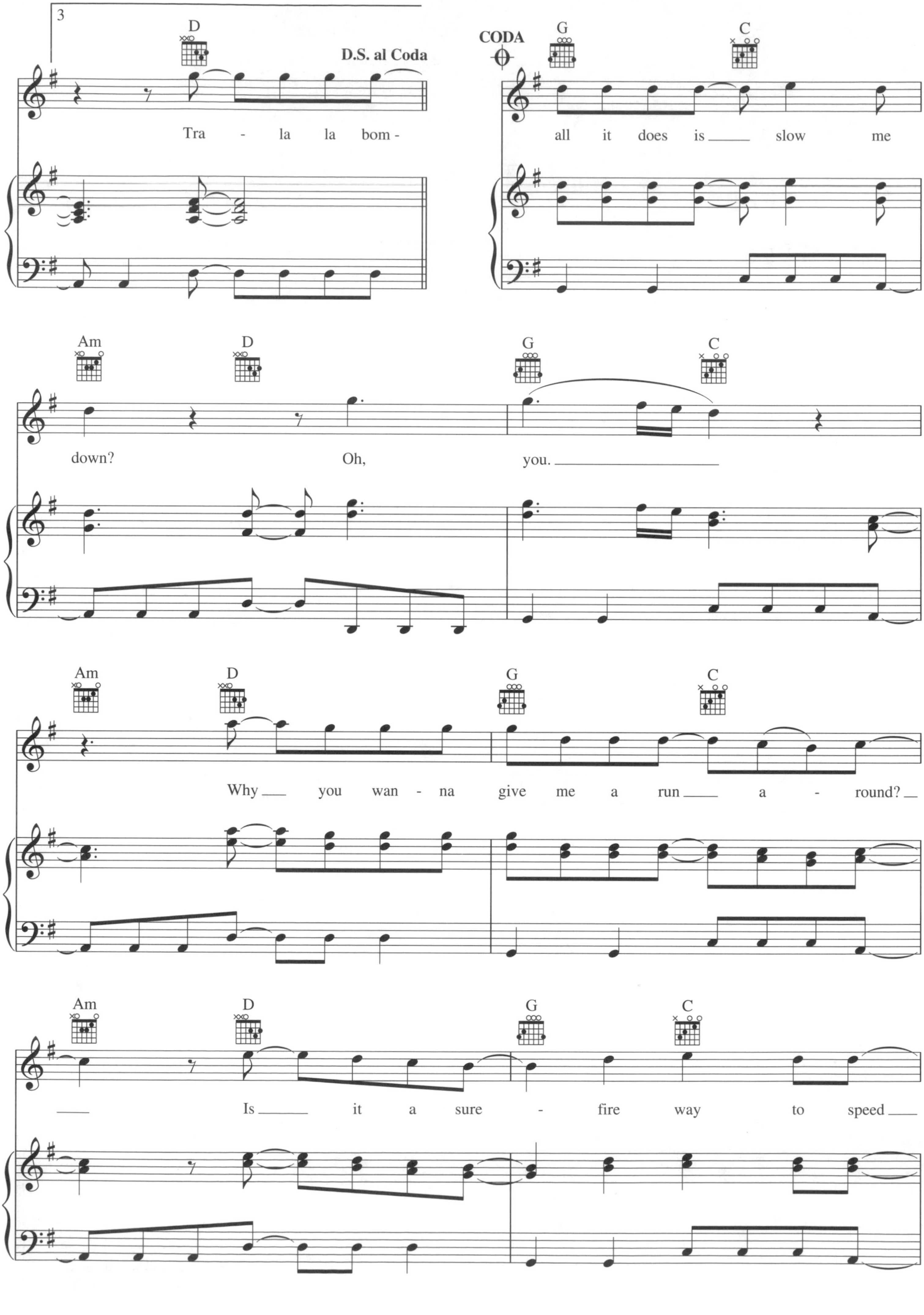

3
D
D.S. al Coda
Tra - la la bom -
CODA
G
C
all it does is slow me
Am
D
G
C
down? Oh, you.
Am
D
G
C
Why you wan - na give me a run a - round?
Am
D
G
C
Is it a sure - fire way to speed

SILENT LUCIDITY

Words and Music by
CHRIS DeGARMO

*1st time vocal is sung one octave lower than written.

am smil-ing next to you ____ in

si - lent lu - cid - i - ty. _____

(Spoken:) Visualize your dreams.   Record it in the present tense.   Put it into a permanent form.

If you persist in your efforts,   you can achieve dream control...

D.S. al Coda
(take 2nd ending)

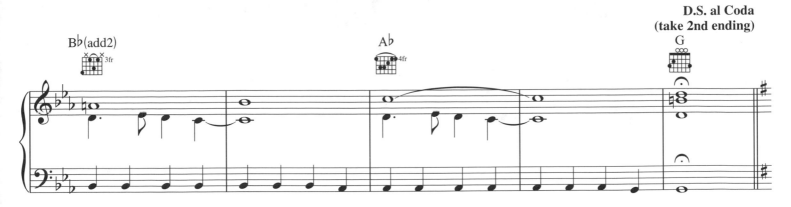

smil - ing next to you. ____

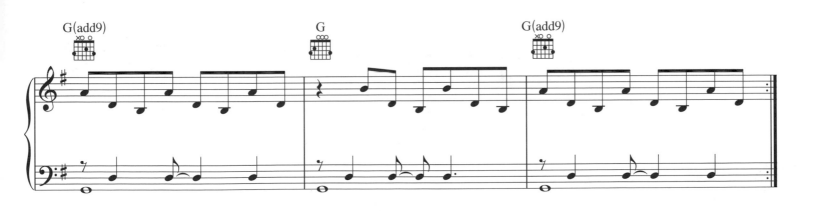

SMELLS LIKE TEEN SPIRIT

Words and Music by KURT COBAIN,
KRIST NOVOSELIC and DAVE GROHL

A♭5 D♭5 F5 B♭5 A♭5 D♭5
4fr 4fr 4fr 4fr
- g'rous. Here we are now; en - ter - tain us. I feel stu -
F5 B♭5 A♭5 D♭5 F5 B♭5
4fr 4fr
- pid and con - ta - gious. Here we are now; en - ter - tain
A♭5 D♭5 F5 B♭5 A♭5 D♭5
4fr 4fr 4fr 4fr
To Coda
us. A mu - lat - to, an al - bi - no, a mos - qui -
F5 B♭5 A♭5 D♭5 F5 E5 F5 G♭5
4fr 4fr
N.C.
- to, my li - bi - do. Yeah! Oy.

UNDER THE BRIDGE

Words and Music by ANTHONY KIEDIS, FLEA,
JOHN FRUSCIANTE and CHAD SMITH

Some-times I feel ____ like I
drive on her streets ____ 'cause
hard to be - lieve ____ that there's

don't have a part - ner.
she's my com - pan - ion. I
no - bod - y out ____ there. It's

Some-times I feel ____ like
walk through her hills 'cause she
hard to be - lieve ____ that

347

CODA

take me all the way, _____ yeah, _____ yeah, _____ yeah. _____

Oh, _____ no _____ no no, _____ yeah, _____ yeah. _____

Love _____ me, _____ I said, _____ yeah, _____ yeah. _____

One time. _____ Un-der the bridge _____ down-town

349

STAY

Words and Music by
LISA LOEB

SUPERSTAR

Written by LAURYN HILL
With Additional Lyrical Contribution
by JOHARI NEWTON and Additional Musical
Contribution by JAMES POYSER

(Spoken:) Yo, hip-hop started out in the heart, uh-huh, yo. Now everybody tryin' to chart. Say what?

Hip-hop started out in the heart, yo, uh. Now everybody tryin' to chart. C' - mon

now, ba-by. C'-mon now, ba-by. C'-mon now, ba-by. C'-mon. Woo. C' - mon

Additional Lyrics

Rap: I cross sands in distant lands, made plans with the sheiks.
Why you beef with freaks as my album sales peak?
All I wanted was to sell like 500
And be a ghetto superstar since my first album, *Blunted.*
I used to work at Foot Locker, they fired me and fronted.
Or I quitted, now I spit it—however do you want it?
Now you get it!
Writing rhymes my range with the frames slightly tinted.
Then send it to your block and have my full name cemented.
And if your rhymes sound like mine, I'm taking a percentage.
Unprecedented and still respected when it vintage.
I'm serious, I'm taking over areas in Aquarius.
Running red lights with my 10,000 chariots.
Just as Christ was a superstar, you stupid star.
They'll hail you then they'll nail you, no matter who you are.
They'll make you now then take you down.
And make you face it, if you slit the bag open.
And put your pinky in it, then taste it.

THAT THING YOU DO!

from the Original Motion Picture Soundtrack THAT THING YOU DO!

Words and Music by
ADAM SCHLESINGER

THIS KISS

Words and Music by ANNIE ROBOFF,
BETH NIELSEN CHAPMAN and ROBIN LERNER

TWO PRINCES

Words and Music by
SPIN DOCTORS

WALKING IN MEMPHIS

Words and Music by
MARC COHN

YOU'RE STILL THE ONE

Words and Music by SHANIA TWAIN
and R.J. LANGE

ZOOT SUIT RIOT

Words and Music by
STEVE PERRY

Recorded a half step lower.